# Black Girls Heal

## MINDFULNESS COLORING BOOK

### BY SHENA TUBBS, M.MFT, LPC

### ILLUSTRATED BY LAUREN SEVILLA

Black Girls Heal: Mindfulness Coloring Book
by Shena Tubbs, M.MFT, LPC
Illustrated by Lauren Sevilla

Copyright © 2018 Shena Tubbs, M.MFT, LPC
www.blackgirlsheal.org

All rights reserved.

Copying, duplicating, or distributing this material electronically or physically for personal use or other self-interests is strictly prohibited unless you have received written permission from the author.

Illustrations by Lauren Sevilla www.lsgraphicshtx.com

For more information and other queries, contact info@blackgirlsheal.org.

Copyright © 2018 Shena Tubbs
All rights reserved.

ISBN-10: 1985303809
ISBN-13: 978-1985303805

# DEDICATION

*To my late mother and beautiful sisters...*

*May your healing journeys in this life and the next be full and complete.*

# TABLE OF CONTENTS

**Introduction to Black Girls Heal**
**The Healing Power of Coloring**
**How to Use this Book**

**Sections**
*Healing*
*Spirit*
*Celebration*
*Power*
*Purpose*

**Appendix**
*Resources*
*Acknowledgments*
*About the Author*

# INTRODUCTION

In the journey towards emotional healing, it can be hard for women of color to find support that they feel represents them and gives practical steps towards healing.

A self help book here.

A therapy session there.

It's common to try to piece meal healing together.

It can feel daunting to break free and make sense of it all. Thus, we remain aware of inner aches that prayer, yoga, financial success, etc., can't really seem to reach.

## THE MISSION...

Black Girls Heal grew out of the desire to bridge this gap by giving accessible, practical mental health coaching and self help tools to women of color who have encountered trauma during their developmental years. As children, these hurtful experiences have helped to shape our perspectives and sense of self worth for better or for worse.

For some, it can be jarring to say what we went through was "trauma," almost as if it was a slight to the caregivers and guardians we love. We may have grown accustomed to explaining away why our feelings were not important while still carrying the weight of what happened. We know they tried their best, thus there is an urge to excuse and rationalize the past with statements like:

*It was my fault.*

*I'm just too sensitive.*

*Everyone goes through bad times, and
I just need to move on.*

For others, the term "trauma" is accurate and validating. What happened to us was earth-shattering and unsettling. We grew up knowing that what we saw and experienced wasn't right, and we may have felt powerless at times to stop it. As a result, our perspectives, self-image, and relationships with others were affected - often to the detriment of our ability to be open and trust.

To heal, first we have to put a name to what happened with us, starting by calling it what it is and was: trauma.

## ABOUT TRAUMA...

Examples of childhood trauma include:

- Emotional neglect
- Verbal abuse
- Physical abuse
- Sexual abuse
- Narcissistic abuse
- Emotional incest
- Abandonment trauma
- Grief trauma
- Addiction in the family
- Medical trauma
- Untreated mental illness by caregivers

These issues are common and rampant, yet we don't often talk about them. We are told that "what happens in this house, stays in this house," which leads to isolation. However, no matter how sophisticated the defense mechanisms, unaddressed trauma gets stored in our bodies and comes out in some manner.

Our pain may have manifested in varied forms like anger, chaotic relationships, anxiety, depression, sexualizing our feelings, drug use, eating disorders, workaholicism, perfectionism, etc. Some of our coping mechanisms may look functional and healthy on the outside, but there's still the wound underneath.

Unfortunately, as people of color, we are prone to be exposed to even more forms of trauma based on systemic and inherited racism. Examples of these traumas include:

- Community violence
- Criminalization & discrimination
- Poverty trauma
- Self image trauma and colorism

\* \* \* \* \*

Repetitive, consistent exposure to multiple traumatic events throughout childhood impacts our self-esteem, sense of safety, and ability to trust our environment and others. Often, this trauma may show up in our bodies as well in sicknesses such as gastrointestinal problem, heart issues, etc. Unfortunately, if we do not find an outlet for the pain, it will work to release itself.

## A WAY OUT...

It may seem daunting, but healing is possible!! It's also necessary and our birthright.

To break the chain of generational trauma and the effects that systemic racism can and does have on little black girls who become adult black women, we must begin the healing process by returning to ourselves.

This book is one of many first steps one can take to engage and begin the process, and I'm happy you're here!

# THE HEALING POWER OF COLORING

This coloring book is one of many tools used by the Black Girls Heal Trauma Recovery School (found at blackgirlsheal.org) to help educate about the effects of childhood trauma and create new patterns of self care, healing, and healthy mindfulness.

Coloring, specifically, connects us back to our childhood. Often times, our inner child has been silenced or is hurting. We create different defense mechanisms to make sure she (our inner child) is okay and thriving though we are not. From overworking to overcompensating, we forget how to play.

Because we forget how to play, the vulnerability and openness that is grown and cultivated through childhood is often repressed as we look for "safer" forms of expression.

As Black Women, we are celebrated for being strong and resilient and rarely get a chance to relax and be vulnerable, open, and, in a way, free. May this book help you reclaim some of that if needed!

This book is to be used to teach you how to play again. To be used meditatively to connect to yourself and lovingly detach from the stressors of this life. Pictures of adult women of color are intentionally used to help us create connection from the actions of our inner little girls and the women we have become.

# HOW TO USE THIS BOOK

In this book, you will find 25 drawings that celebrate our beauty, heal-ing process, and resilience.

The drawings are grouped into 5 sections. Each one has a blurb and journal prompts for self discovery.

Each drawing is on its own sheet for you to either keep within the book or pull out to hang or show off.

(Note: If you do so on social media, make sure to tag us!)

Use this book when feeling agitated, detached, or even happy! Find colors that speak to you, be they bold and bright or mute and subdued. This is your process, Love.

After you finish all the drawings, if you want more tools to help you in your healing journey, flip to the appendix to learn more!

# HEALING IS YOUR BIRTHRIGHT

# Healing

# RESTORED AND WHOLE

In this journey, the goal is that you be returned to your former self in better shape than where you started.

Wounds healed.

Promises come to fruition.

You finally see the reasons behind the "No's."

Restoration can start today.

## JOURNAL PROMPTS

- What are the places you may have been hurt that need to be r estored?
- What would wholeness feel like to you?
- When has been a time that you felt close to this feeling? What got in the way?

# BONDAGE BREAKER

Trauma bonds occur in relationships where there is a combination of intense emotions, inconsistency, confusion, and a promise (said or imagined) of love and connection. You stay because you are holding on for that promise as it may fulfill a deep need inside of you. As a result, you may tolerate infidelity, abuse, toxicity, and shaming.

Soul ties and trauma bonds keep us bound, but therapy and recovery can help us get better. We can be free from the relationships, the pain, and memories of our past.

## JOURNAL PROMPTS

- What relationships you may think qualify/qualified as a trauma bond relationship?
- What promise are/were you holding on for?
- What fears get in the way of letting go?

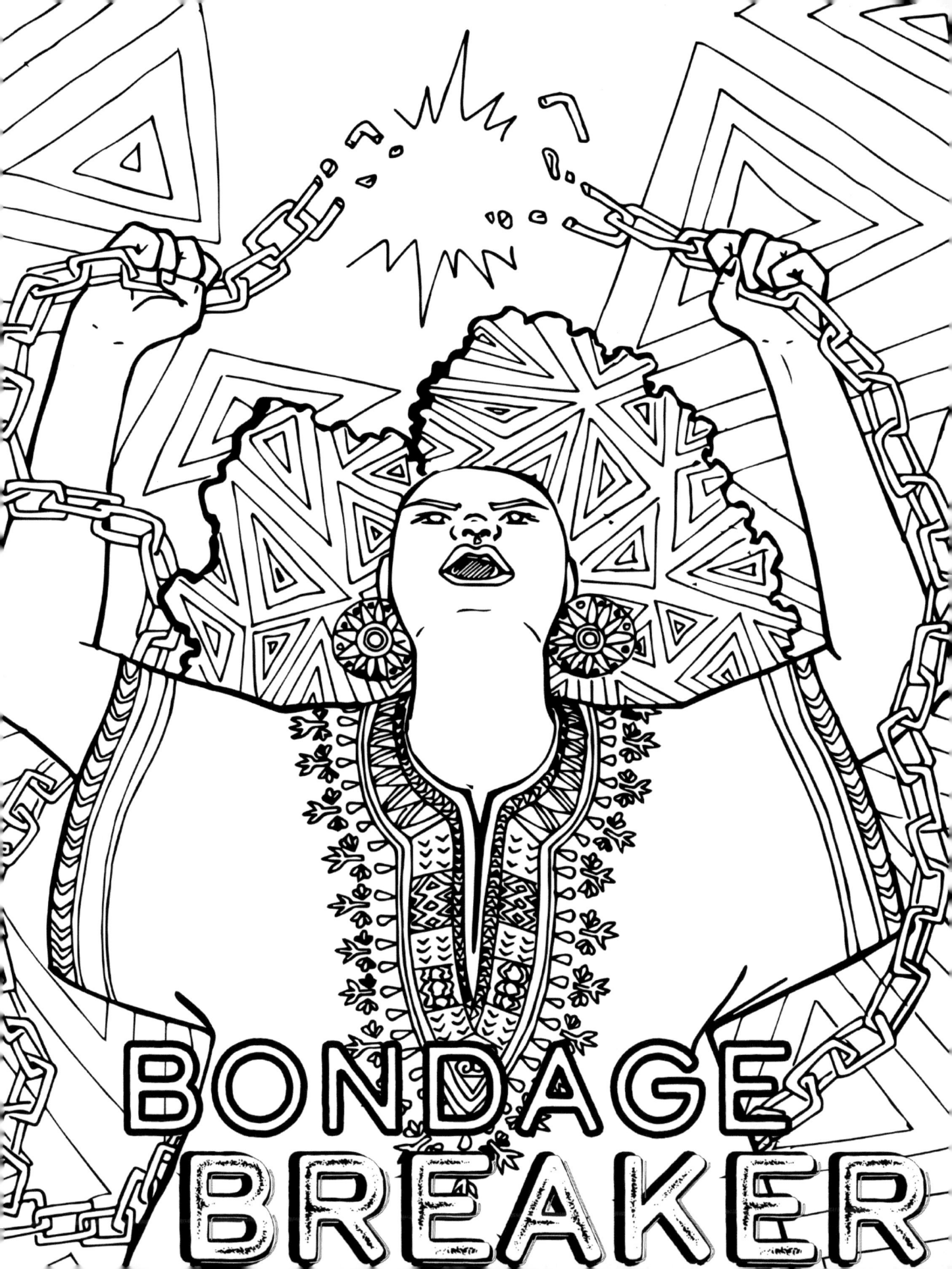

# VULNERABILITY

It is a common defense mechanism to keep walls up and people out. However, when you keep people out, good experiences, hope and love also cannot get in. There is an unending cycle of believing the world is unsafe and untrustworthy. As a result, healthy individuals are not allowed in to prove otherwise.

Allow yourself to be "seen" so that you can be fully at home within your body and with others.

On the other side of this vulnerability is where you find true self acceptance.

## JOURNAL PROMPTS

- How would you describe your level of vulnerability?
- What makes it difficult to be vulnerable? Easier?
- With whom have you been holding back that you need to practice vulnerability?

# PEACE

One of the key signs that you are making progress in your healing journey is the presence of peace.

Peace is not ignoring situations and stuffing down uncomfortable feelings while repeating positive mantras and affirmations.

Peace is the inner knowing and felt sense that everything will be okay. When triggered, you're able to notice it and move on without going into defense mode nor putting your head in the sand.

There is strength in peace to overcome life's difficulties.

## JOURNAL PROMPTS

- How would you describe peace for you? How do you know if you are in a state of peace?
- What obstacles or hurdles get in the way of your peace?
- What have you done to move towards peace? If nothing, what can you start today?

# FORGIVENESS

Forgiveness is imperative for our healing. We are held hostage when we allow the sins and ills of others to hold fast to us. Many times those who hurt us carry on with their lives unbothered, while we are the ones laid out in the wreckage.

Forgiveness does not mean that you condone what happened to you, but it means you are ready to be free of it. You can move on and not have to bear this burden any more.

# JOURNAL PROMPTS

- What do you believe about forgiveness? Should it be earned or given?
- Has forgiveness helped you in the past? Why or why not?
- Who are those you need to forgive?
- Are there any ills or mistakes you must forgive yourself for?

# CONNECTION TO THAT GREATER THAN OURSELVES OFFERS SPACE FOR HEALING

# Spirit

# PRAYER

Contact with your Higher Power is transformational and healing. The ability to surrender and connect to something outside of yourself allows you to know you do not have to fix everything yourself, nor do you have to understand it.

Prayer and meditation have scientifically proven benefits of stress relief and are indicators of emotional health.

Seek to have a daily practice of meditation, prayer, or another mindfulness activity to build clarity, awareness, and peace in your life.

# JOURNAL PROMPTS

- Do you have a daily prayer or mindfulness practice? If so, how has it served you?
- Are there any blocks keeping you from building this practice?
- Are there any holes you feel these practices don't fill or complete within yourself?

# BLESSED

In all things, there is still positivity and hope. If you look for evidence of blessing, you will find it—whether it be life and breath, a career, a family member or dear friend, or any combination of the above.

If you are weighed down by the calamities of life, start to break free by beginning to count your blessings.

## JOURNAL PROMPTS

- Are there any barriers keeping you from being able to feel blessed or see your blessings?
- Do you ever battle guilt that you do not "feel" blessed?
- Can you list out items that you would call blessings?

# OPENNESS

Like vulnerability, openness is allowing yourself to be available to change. Without openness, you are closed off, and when goodness comes your way, you won't be able to receive it.

If you struggle with allowing yourself to be open, do not feel ashamed. Along the way, you learned it was safer to remain cautious in life to avoid being hurt.

Thankfully, just like we learned to not trust those around us or positive experiences (for threat of being disappointed), we can unlearn these beliefs and behaviors as well.

## JOURNAL PROMPTS

- How would you describe how open you are to new experiences? To new relationships?
    - If guarded, what holds you back?
- Have you had an experience where you were hesitant, but practiced openness and the result was positive?
- What is one way you can practice openness this week?

# STRENGTH

India Aire said it best. You have had them inside of you all along. Allow yourself to tap into your intuition and trust that still small voice inside of you. You may have lost your recognition of it if you have spent time listening to the voices of caregivers and loved ones, friends, bosses, society, and institutions... but I promise you, it's still there.

Once you reconnect to your inner strength, reinforce to yourself that you are strong and powerful. You are resilient. It is okay to walk in that and own your power.

## JOURNAL PROMPTS

- How strong do you feel daily? If regularly, do you feel your strength comes from a defensive place, a place of self-empowerment, or both?
- What would it look like to be strong?
- Where and when are the times you allow yourself to not be strong? If few or none, why is that?

# WISDOM

Wisdom is the ability to take accumulated knowledge and apply it to experiences to make productive decisions and judgments. Notice, I used the word "productive" versus "bad."

All of our experiences teach us, thus there is no such thing as a "bad" decision or judgment as long as we aim to learn from them.

Take every moment and experience and invite your intuition and Higher Power to be a part of it to help guide you to the right action.

# JOURNAL PROMPTS

- How would you describe your connection to your inner wisdom?
- Who are people you admire who are wise? What qualities show their wisdom?

Wisdom

# WE ARE BEAUTIFUL.
# WE ARE UNIQUE.
# WE ARE IMPORTANT.

# Celebration

# MAGICAL

We all have magic within us to call the things that are unseen into the now.

What we speak we will possess and what we touch turns gold.

Own your power and magic, my dear. Walk in it.

Your black is beautiful and perfectly made.

# JOURNAL PROMPTS

- Who are your favorite "Magical Black Girls" and why?
- What are things that you celebrate about your blackness? If you do not (or it's difficult), what gets in the way?

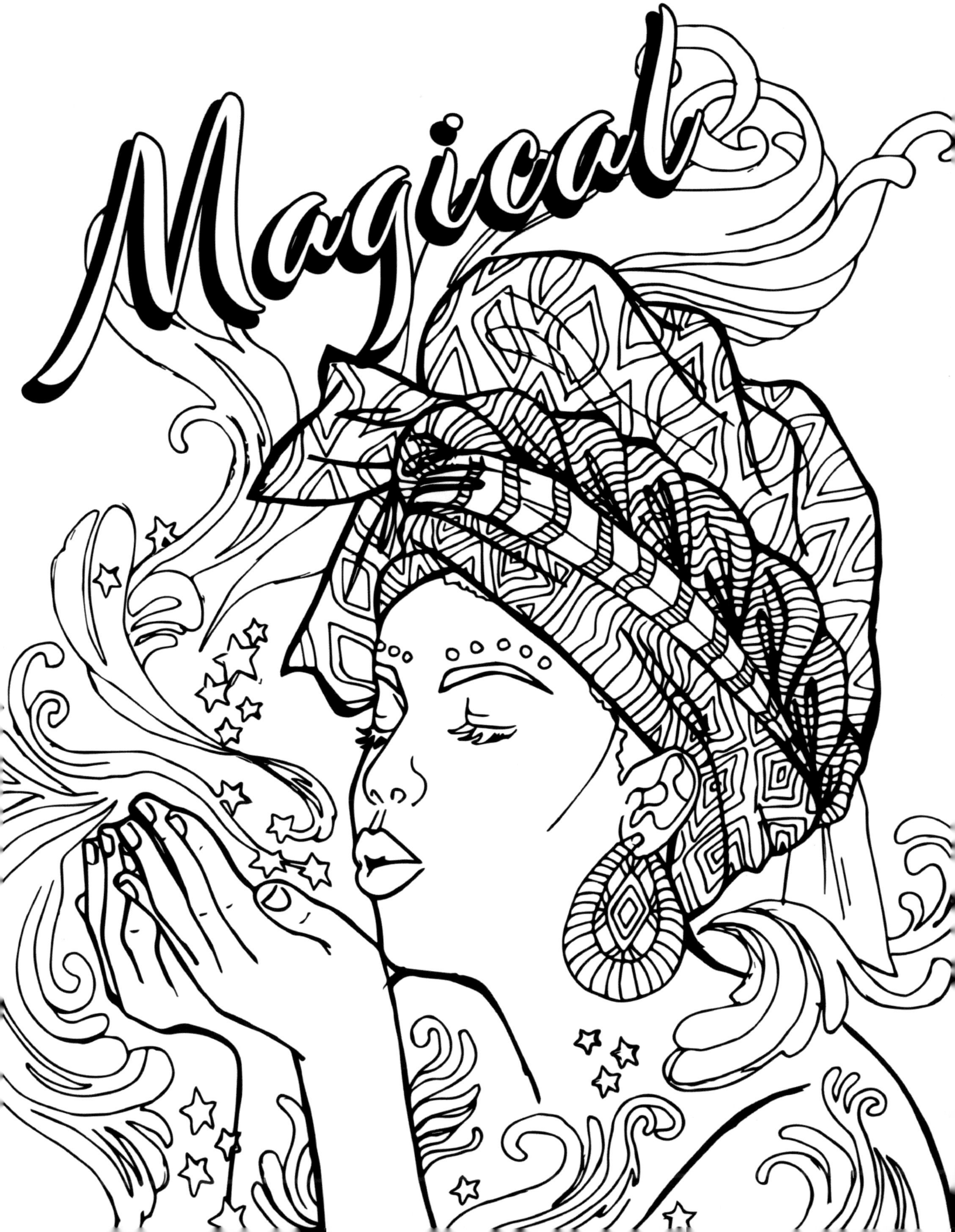
Magical

# SLAYED TO THE GODS

Beauty is a natural gift given to all of God's creation. When we are engage in self care practices and revel in our own beauty, we are honoring God. Slaying doesn't have to incorporate makeup and adornments, but rather owning the entirety of who we are with love and gratitude.

Owning every curve, every freckle, and every curl with confidence that we ARE made perfectly.

## JOURNAL PROMPTS

- What self practices do you like to engage in the best?
- Describe your journey towards acceptance of your appearance.

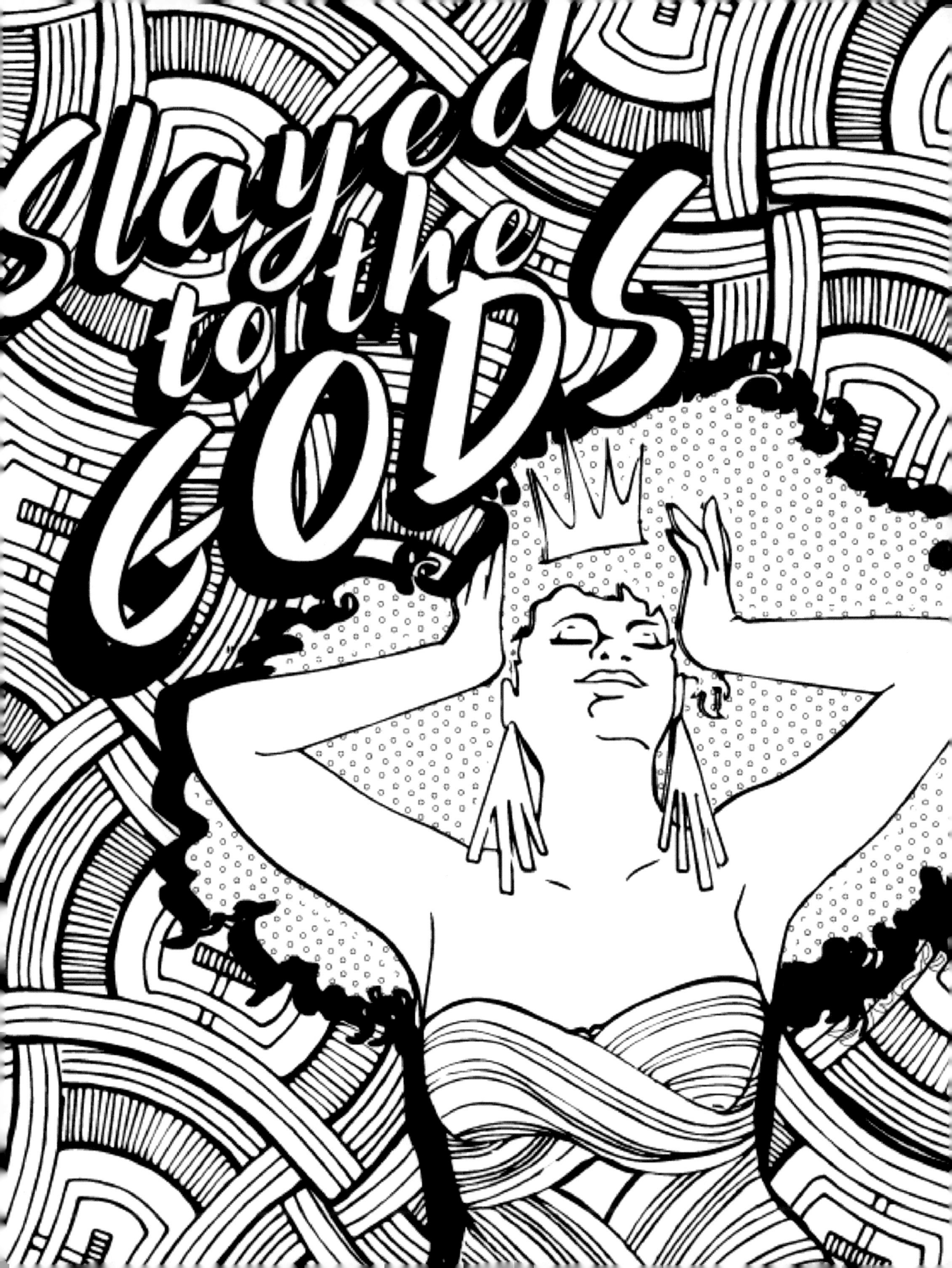
Slayed
to the
GODS

# SELF LOVE

It's common for those of us with trauma to swing in two different directions when it comes to self love. On one end we swing to denying ourselves and taking care of others to gain their love. On the other spectrum, we are fiercely defensive of anyone who would try to demean or take advantage of us. We're afraid the pain would reinforce that fear that we are not good enough.

Self love is the deep knowing that we are good enough, pretty enough, smart enough. We are wanted. We are strong. And because we are inherently all of these things, we love ourselves. Love is from the inside out.

## JOURNAL PROMPTS

- How would you describe your relationship with yourself?
- If self love is an area of growth, what practices or beliefs would you hope to have?
- What is the best bit of advice you have received on how to build and cultivate self love?

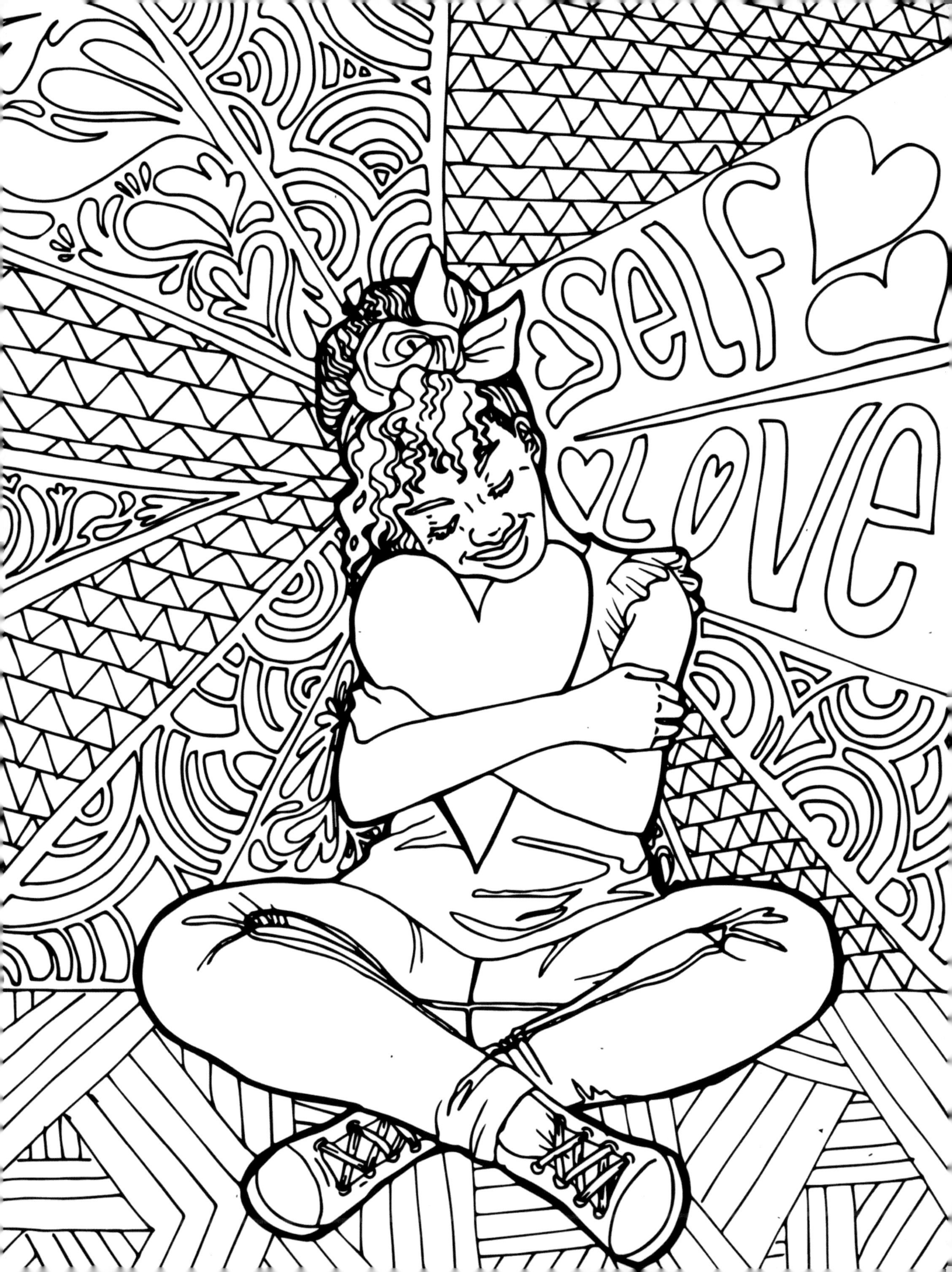
SELF
LOVE

# UNBOTHERED

There is a difference between avoiding our problems and remaining unbothered. To be unbothered means that we are resilient. That we allow the circumstances of life to roll of our back because the ultimate power lies within us.

We give our power both to problems and others when we worry, doubt, and stress. Because we know who we are and whose we are, we do not stress when someone does not like us or a circumstance does not go our way.

We use positive thinking and mindsets to reframe what is going on to persist, overcome, and thrive.

## JOURNAL PROMPTS

- Would you say you are deeply affected by the thoughts and opinions of others? Why or why not?
- Would you say you are deeply affected by life circumstances that may seem impossible?
- What perspective change(s) do you think may need to make to feel "unbothered"?

# Unbothered

# YAAS

"yaas" /yas/

*exclamation*

1. Statement of jubilation, excitement and glee.
2. Statement of approval and agreement,

*synonyms: "You go girl", "I'm impressed", "I love it", "I'm proud of you"*

## JOURNAL PROMPTS

- Name three people, things, or situations that make you want to go "Yaaasss!"
- Who are your cheerleaders? How do they encourage you?
- How do you cheerlead? How do you encourage them?

Yaas!

# YOU ALREADY HAVE EVERYTHING YOU NEED INSIDE OF YOU

Power

# SURVIVOR

We are survivors.

As black people, we have overcome systemic oppression, genocides, wars, drug epidemics, diseases and various other injustices to burst through and survive not only intact, but whole.

As a resilient people, we thrive and will overcome.

## JOURNAL PROMPTS

- To you, what does it mean to be a survivor?
- What is the difference between thriving and surviving? Where do you feel you lay in that?
- What factors have helped you be resilient from your past?

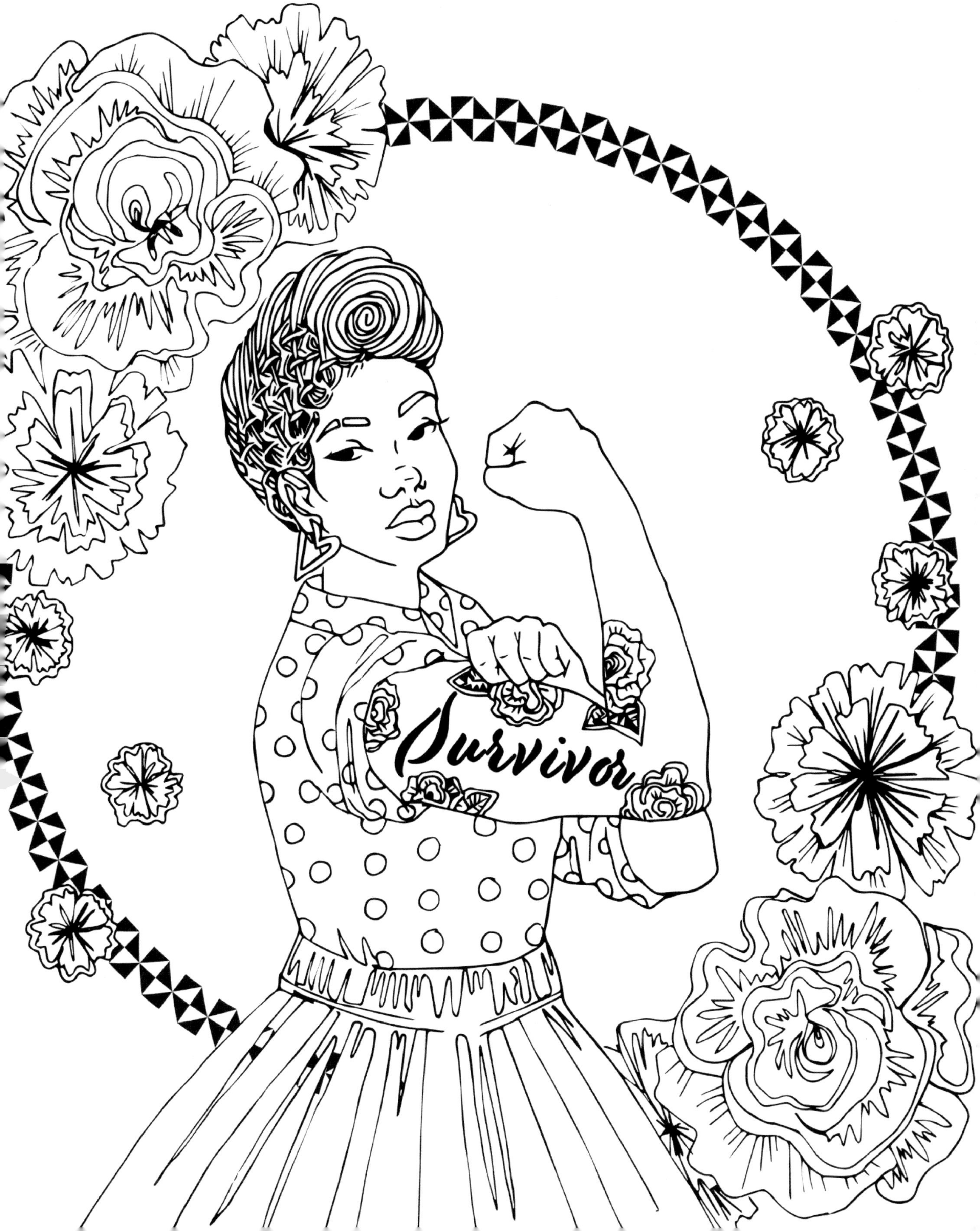
Survivor

# EMPOWERED

When we walk in our power, there is a strength following it. Empowerment is having the knowledge that you are able, capable, and strong enough to do the thing you set out to do. You do not have to be bound by previous circumstances or unhealthy mindsets.

Today, you can break free and move on.

# JOURNAL PROMPTS

- What comes to mind when you see the "Empowered" coloring page?
- What is your source of power?
- How do you express your power? If you feel this is a place for growth, how would you like to express your power?

Empowered

# YES, I CAN

You can do it, girl. Whatever you are struggling with. Whatever you are second guessing. Whatever your hesitation, keep going. You got this.

You already have everything you need inside of you. You don't have to wait for permission from others or their validation. It's in you, so go for it!

## JOURNAL PROMPTS

- Name a current circumstance or hurdle that feels very lofty and there is doubt you can achieve it. Why do you feel that way?
- Name one time you did something that felt impossible, but you made it through.
- Now list another obstacle that you conquered that felt impossible.
- How do you feel now about the original problem above? If still anxious, what resources do you need to solve the problem?

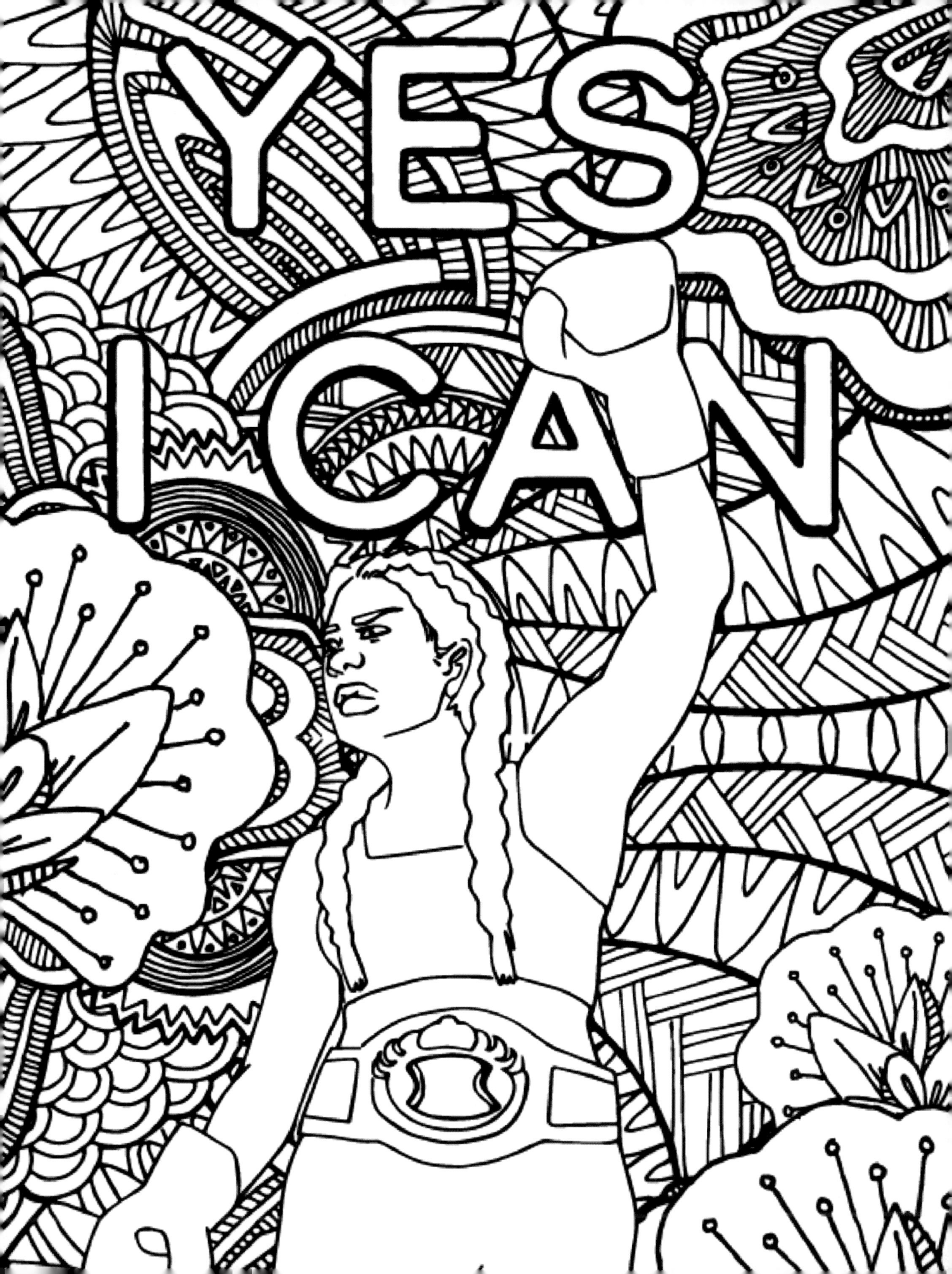
YES
I CAN

# UNSTOPPABLE

The only person who can stop you is you.

Not circumstances...

Not "the man"

Not family and friends...

You have the power to make a change. Do it today, right now, in this moment.

# JOURNAL PROMPTS

- List or describe the things you fight against (i.e. thoughts, emotions, people, memories, obstacles)

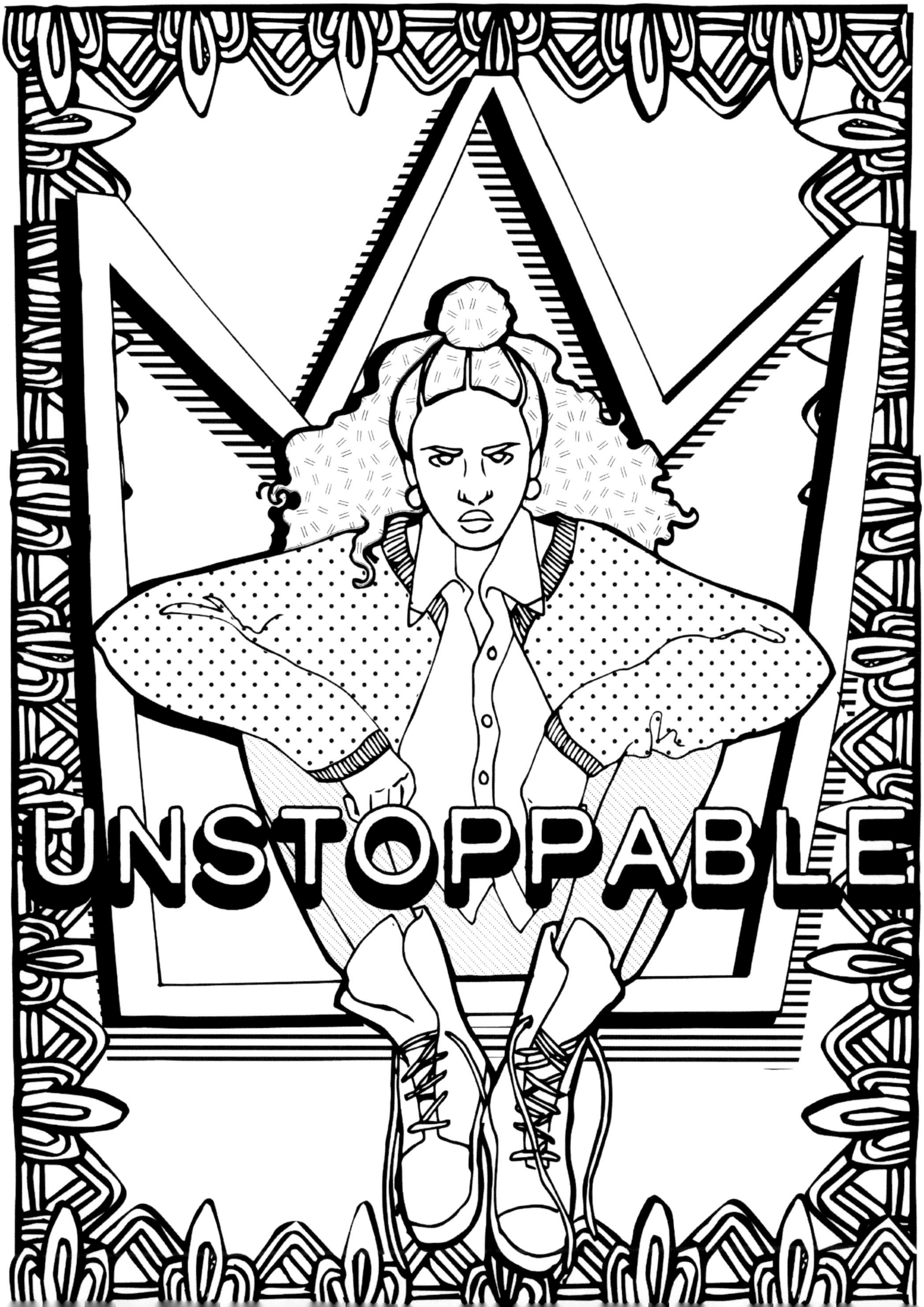
UNSTOPPABLE

# PUSH ON

The trials of life can get overwhelming and seemingly hard to conquer. You have a choice about whether you want to push on or remain stagnant.

Sometimes the only way out of a situation is through it.

## JOURNAL PROMPTS

- What are mantras or statements you say to yourself to help you keep going when feeling discouraged?
- Would you describe those statements as positive or negative?
- Who in your life would say those things to you growing up? Were they positive or negative influences?

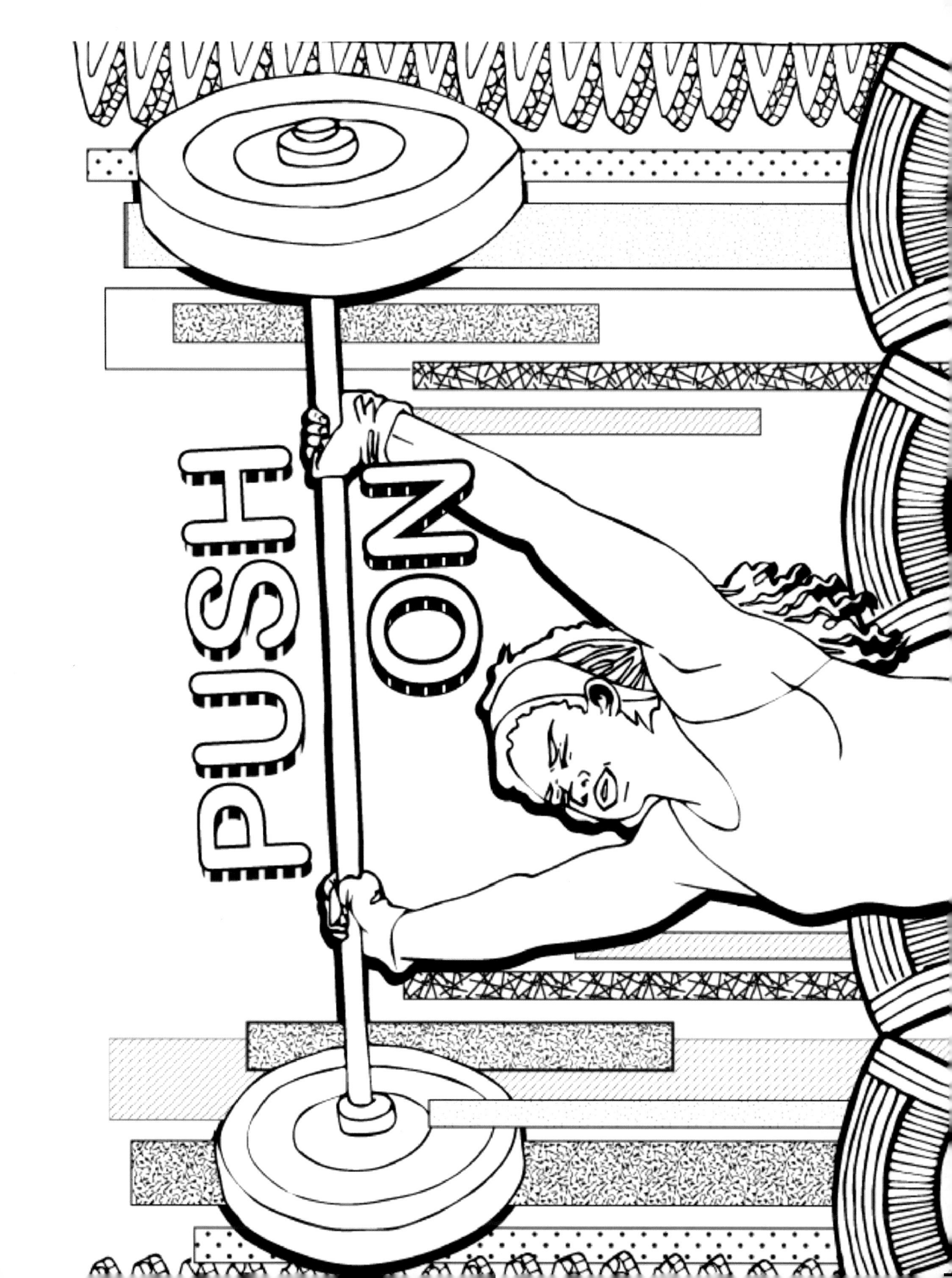

PUSH ON

# WE ARE ALL BUILT TO DO SOMETHING AMAZING.

# Purpose

# LIFE IS DOPE

Life is full of amazing treasures and opportunities. Because we are still here, there is still the opportunity to change and grow. There is a choice in every circumstance about how to see an experience – two lens we can see through – positive and negative.

Today, revel in the majesty that is life. Revel in the opportunity given to you today to overcome and make the most of the moment. Make meaning out of everything that is happening to you. And always always give yourself permission to find the joy.

## JOURNAL PROMPTS

- List 3-5 positive things happening in your life around you.
- List three negative situations or problems. Notice if you can find the "bright side" or a positive reasons or lesson why this may be happening.

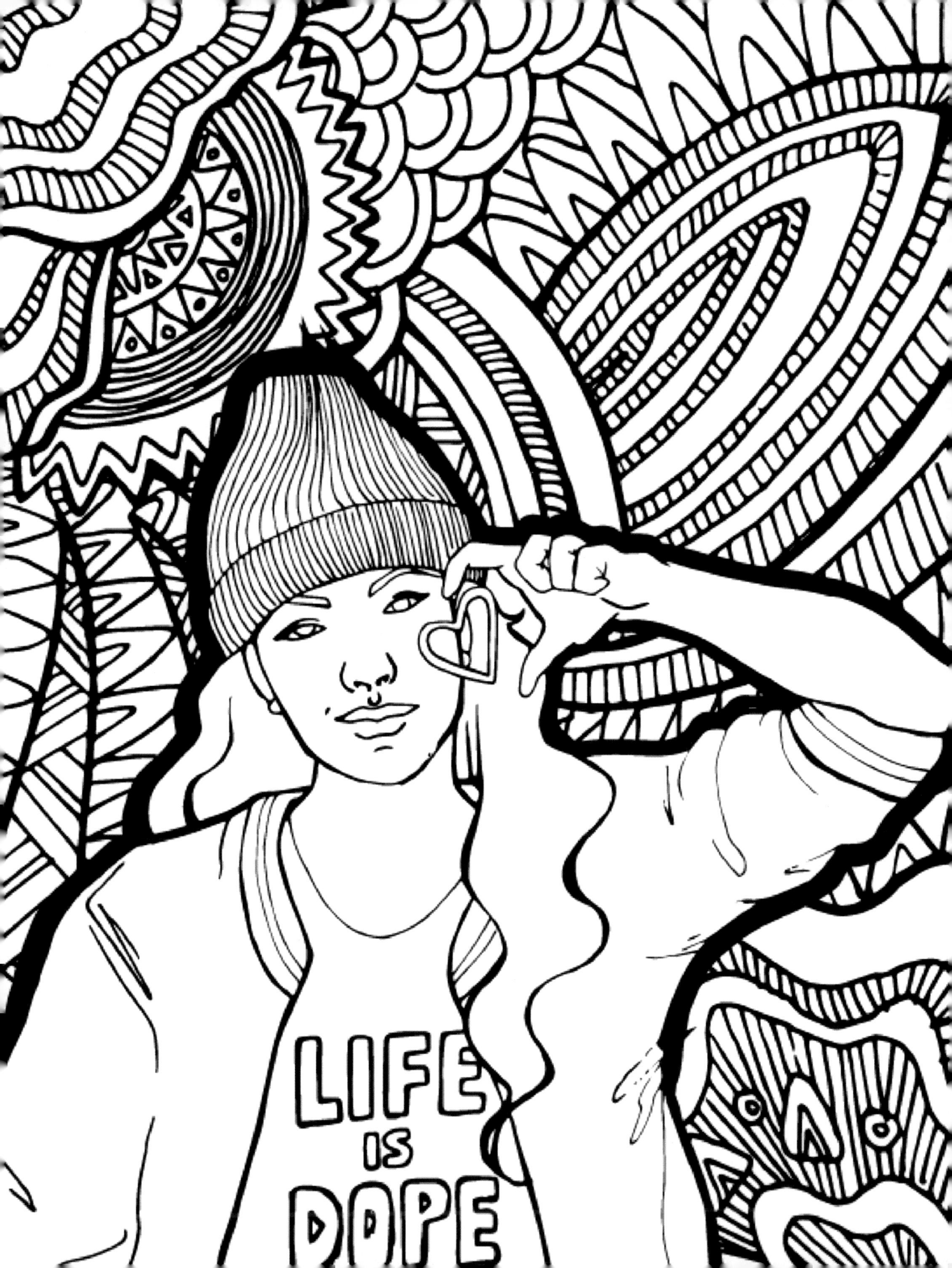
LIFE
IS
DOPE

# THE STORY ISN'T OVER

Our lives are like a story, full of different chapters and addendums. Because you are still here, you have the opportunity to create another story. You can close today's chapter and start anew. This doesn't negate the previous parts of your story or act like they don't exist, because that's part of what has brought you to this place. However, you are the author of your story, and you can write something anew.

## JOURNAL PROMPTS

- How would you describe the "chapters" in your life so far? What would you title them?
- How would you like your next chapter of your life to look? What would you title it? What actions are you taking to get there?

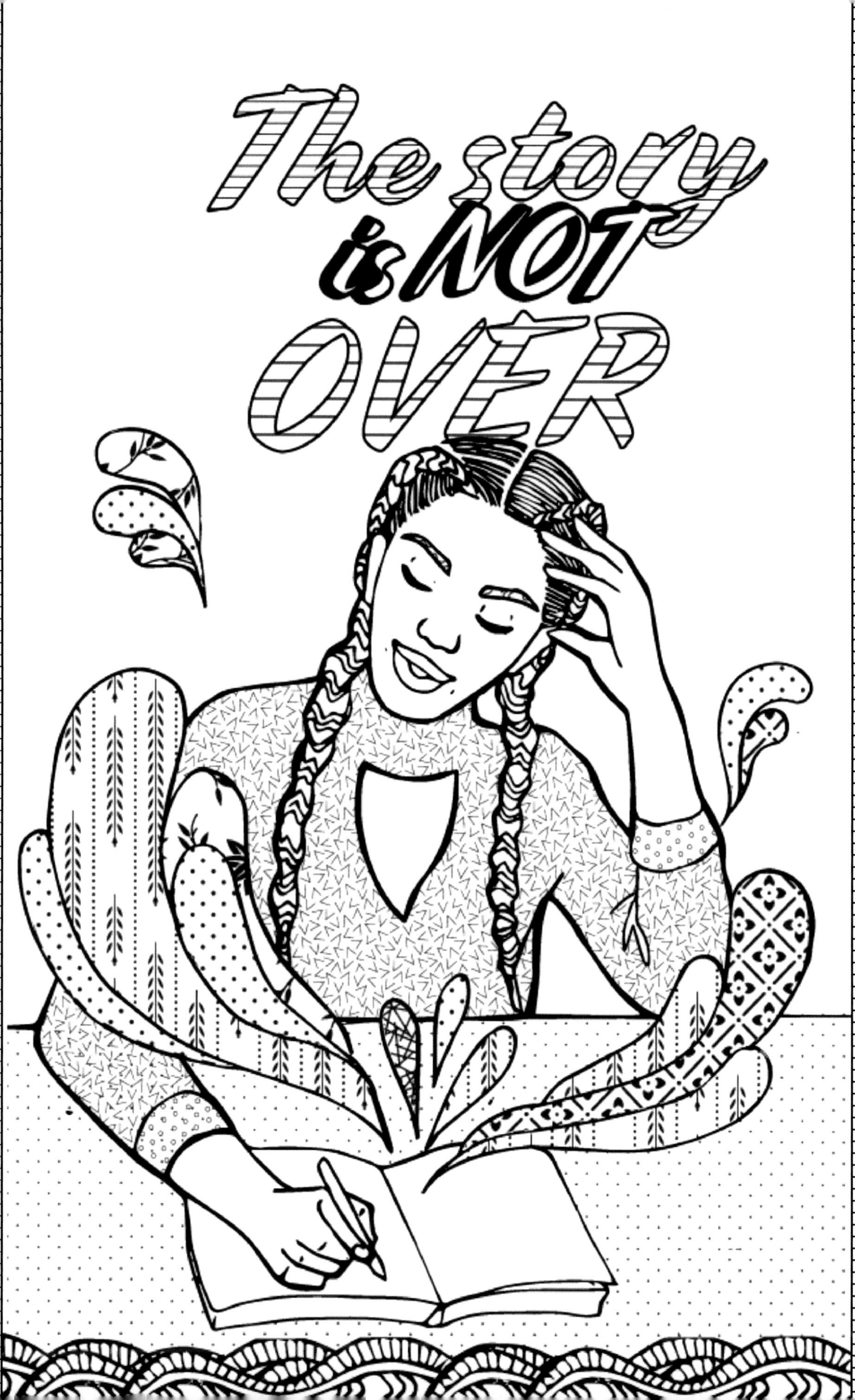
The story
is NOT
OVER

# THRIVE

You are not just a survivor, my dear. You are a Thriver! You are built for so much more... bigger and better things, and they are coming.

Believe and they will be here!

# JOURNAL PROMPTS

- How do you know when you're not just surviving, but thriving?
- Is the success that you have or are working towards based on your definition or the definition or others? If not your own, what needs to change for you to make it your best life worth living?

Thrive

# GOAL DIGGER

Keep your eyes on your prize. Your dreams are needed to make this world a better place. Stay focused and carry on.

However, remember that your worth is not determined by how much you achieve or succeed. You are inherently valuable, talented and special. Those are the qualities you bring to your goal, not the other way around.

# JOURNAL PROMPTS

- List the goals you are working towards. Why are they important to you?
- Do you feel valuable when not working towards them or do you feel your value is attached to them in some way?
- How do you stay focused on your goals? Are there any distractions you need to let go?

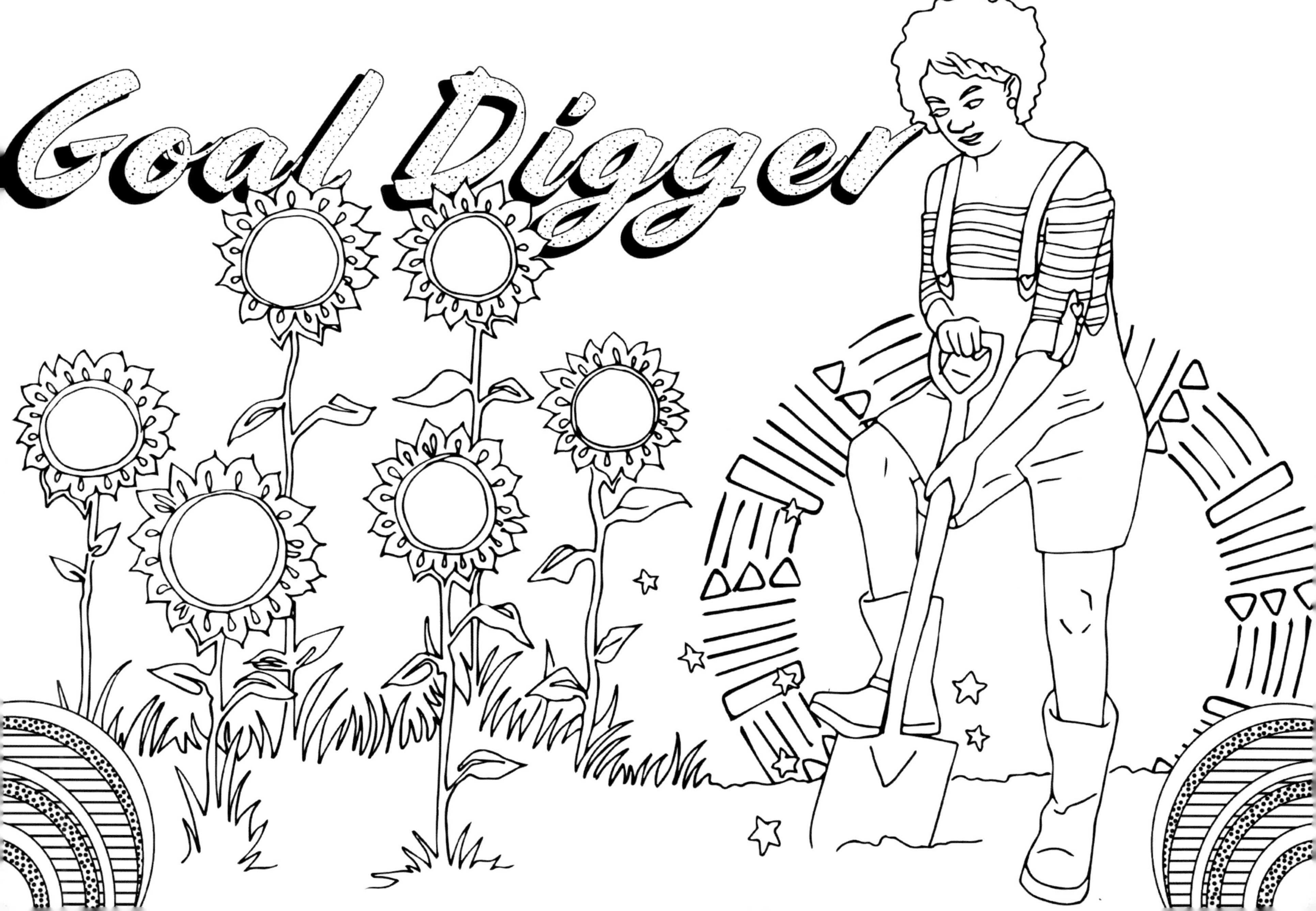
Goal Digger

# REST

You don't need to do it all yourself. You can let go and heal. You can move through and let things happen around you.

You don't have to DO to feel worthy.

You don't have to complete, accomplish, or create.

## JOURNAL PROMPTS

- What are you favorite ways to rest?
- How comfortable are you allowing yourself to rest?
- What steps can you take to protect time and space to allow you to rest (even if it is just an hour)?

# Rest

# FIND HEALING.
# FIND YOUR TRIBE.

# Appendix

# THE ULTIMATE RESOURCE

If you're ready to change your life, perspectives, and relationships, the *Black Girls Heal Trauma Recovery School* is the best resource.

The *Black Girls Heal Trauma Recovery School* is a live 12 week course that personally walks you through emotional triggers, ways to interact with your past hurts, replacement behaviors and actions you can take when feeling unsafe or struggling

Though not a replacement for therapy, you will learn a wide variety of applicable and practical therapeutic tools to use immediately to build self awareness, effective coping strategies, and healing.

It differs from therapy because you will have direct access to your coach for questions, support, and guidance throughout the week and months after the program ends as well!

### As a result of the course you will:

- Be aware of the root sources of pain and next steps
- Learn why you may self sabotage and what to do instead
- Grow skills to use when feeling upset and triggered
- Gain insight on addictive behaviors and compulsions
- Begin the process of healing negative core beliefs
- Build life changing connections within the BGH B-Girl community to spur you on towards healing

Go to BlackGirlsHeal.org to sign up and learn more!

# WANT MORE DRAWINGS?

Visit **BlackGirlsHeal.org** for free digital downloads of brand new coloring pages!

# ACKNOWLEDGEMENTS

A rousing thank you to my illustrator & graphic designer, **Lauren Sevilla.** Your heart for social justice and the empowerment of women of color is palpable. This book literally would not have been possible without you. Thank you for your generosity of spirit.

To **Mari Lee** and my **Like a Boss! crew**. Your encouragement and direction kept me focused. Thanks for pushing me to be the first tangible for the Black Girls Heal community. I so appreciate you.

To **Haley**, thank you for editing this bad boy. You're the best, and I love you dearly.

To **Chela**, my P.I.C.. Thank you for being my cheerleader. You have no idea how much your energy and encouragement has spurred me on. Thanks for believing in me!

To **Karuna** for being my A1 since Day 1. Thank you for being such a wonderful friend and being the first person to tell me I have everything I need inside of me.

To **my loving husband** whom I owe so much and could never repay. Thank you for your unending patience and grace with the long nights and work-filled days. You have supported me in more ways than one. Thanks for seeing me and loving me in all things. I love you to the moon and back.

# ABOUT THE AUTHOR

Shena Tubbs is a Trauma Recovery Coach, Licensed Professional Counselor, and Certified Sex Addiction Therapist Candidate in Houston, TX. She loves helping women recover from childhood trauma, overcome intimacy disorders, and heal from sexually compulsive behaviors and addictions.

When not seeing clients or coaching, Shena can be found hosting her podcast "*Love Junkie*" which focuses on healing and recovery from sex and love addictions and codependency.

She is a Chipotle afficionado and loves recharging by spending time with her husband.

Learn more about Shena, listen to *Love Junkie*, and find more free resources at **shenathetherapist.com**.

Made in the USA
Columbia, SC
13 July 2020